CYNICAL RHYMES

and

LULLABIES

David Synn

ISBN-13: 978-0692614860
(Empty Glass Records)
ISBN-10: 0692614869

Editor:
Eva Xanthopoulos
www.evapoetex.com

Cover Art & Illustrations:
Sharon Lyn Stackpole

www.sharonlyn.com

Author Website: www.davidsynn.com

Dedicated to my lovely wife Missy
whom I adore, cherish, and respect.

TABLE OF CONTENTS

ACKNOWLEDGMENTS

I would like to show my extreme gratitude to Sharon Lyn Stackpole for the illustrations and cover and Chad M. Cardinal for the photography.

I want to also thank my wife Missy for her continued support, patience and understanding while I chase this "pipe dream," and my parents for raising me to be the person I am today.

If you believe, you can achieve.

Peace, love and unity.

-David Synn

Social Media

Infection.
The need to make your words
heard. Opinions clashing,
spewing half-truths,
contradicting parables.

The voice.
Keyboard warrior cry,
chant heard across the world,
One button erases existence,
Absurd.

Information age.
The ignorance displayed,
misquoting and misinterpreting.
Enlightenment—
Cemented in the Dark Ages.

Seasons

The seasons divide
and die. The winter long
and unforgiving.
Summer, the best of friends.

Camaraderie surpassed
by fall turning into spring,
aware only of what material
can be gained.

I watch them disappear
and resurface, leaving
mere traces of true colors.
Convenience.

Cupid's Arrow

Attractive, immaculate,
both flawed and facade.
The hands on the clock
spin faster. Time stops.
An explosion, a spark.

Both defective,
searching for companionship,
Shot by Cupid, an unlikely unity.
Marriage. Time progresses,
both losing interest,
vows remain strong,
hearts in need of mending.

The action of separation
seemed imminent,
Searching the other's soul—
Another arrow, another chance.
Romance.

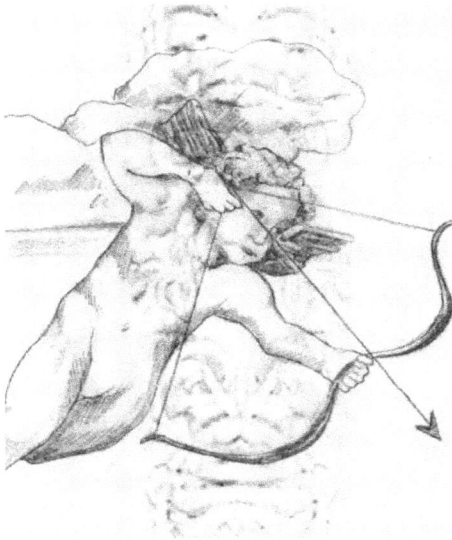

The Recurring Dream

Body hits the floor,
A torso, flailing
its arms wildly,
forcing itself to crawl.

Legs—
Dead weight.
Broken fingernails from dragging
the once-functional meat.

Different scenarios
always ending the same.
On my stomach, alone,
surrendering to the shadows.

Baggage

The ocean, the river
and lake. The oasis
in the desert,
The snake.

The religious fanatic, bigot
and atheist, color blind at birth.
Nothing but bone, hidden
deep within the muscle.

The gay man, straight man
and trans-lesbian,
the heart that bleeds
in them beats for you.

Free yourself of the chains
dragging at your feet.
The snake, coiled, ready to strike—
Epiphany.

Flashy Pretty New God

The savior takes the arena,
carrying the cross,
balancing the weight
on weakened shoulders.

The crowd sings the songs
of the latest deity—
Antichrist;
Flashy pretty new god.

Zombies salivating, meat thrown
in their direction, erratic behavior
of epic proportions. The savior hanging,
wondering why he was forsaken.

Glory Days (The Grandeur of Entitlement)

The accident,
the diagnosis,
the decision to mother
the child or flee,
free.

Teenage melodrama,
French Kissing
an unloaded shotgun,
dumbfounded no one
relates.

Spreading AIDs,
going viral, heads
filled with puss, fluff,
disconnected,
epidemic.

Missy's Song

Lost without your touch,
your guidance leading
me off this island;
My rock.

From where I was
five years ago, to where
I'll be twenty years from now,
I want you on that journey.

Breathing you in,
your essence,
the heat from your body.
Lust.

With the setting sun,
you're there.
Waves crashing into the shore,
My rock, until death do us part.

The Concept

The concept of failing,
a failure in itself.
Unaware of our own
evolutionary progress,
we submit to authority.

Teachers teach us that we
will be anything or nothing.
Both notions irrelevant.
Merit measured by the ability
to move forward.

A primitive idea,
sends mixed messages,
leading men to question their worth.
Contrary, it is only through immense
amount of failure that we know success.

Line in the Sand

Draw a line in the sand,
straight or combined
with the movement of your hand,
in the shape of what you hate,
tracing the wrinkles
on your weathered face.

Draw a line in the sand,
separate the path of the man
you are and the one
standing before you.
Is it violence you seek?
Peace?

The child was 33 years old,
Lines of torment under his
dimming halo. A state of regret
for not knowing his presence,
The feeling of knowledge
that he doesn't exist.

One line can change the world,
taking two or eight,
If they break, replaceable by machines
that think. Computer screens
show stocks crashing,
heart rates fluttering.

A line by itself is just a line,
It can only stretch so far
in your mind. A picture of many
can be sent to any
maximum security guarded island.
Speed of light.

Draw a line in the sand for the sake
of hate or the brotherhood of man.
For religion or to watch it wash
away with the waves.
Only a line—
Everything.

Expiration of Faith

Processed misinformation,
I question the intent,
the continuity. The prophet—
delusional and misguided,
organized to fit the crime.

The scene needs a resurrection;
A crucifixion.
Swiss Bank Accounts assure
the trinity will live forever
in your hearts and your pocketbooks.

Leaping off buildings,
the once-loved verses lose
all meaning. I pour a drink,
reaching a silent revelation.
Freedom.

Cone of Shame

Gravity pulling me down,
puts pressure on bones.
Hairline vanishing,
puts stress on the ego,
Lower jaw swollen shut.

Reflection shows someone
I barely know, needing
my glasses to make the image out.
Wrinkles drawn on.
Peel my skin off.

Cancer eating its way through,
completing the cycle.
Gone are the days of no regrets,
Wearing the cone of shame,
tracing the man on the mirror's surface.

Apathy

The pace,
faster than before.
Sheep falling into place,
hitting every raw nerve
along the way.

The race,
celebrities and chosen
officials, elected by the people.
Red pill, blue pill,
false sense of free will.

Apathetic and hypocritical,
everything will be fine.
We post pictures of our kids
on Facebook, forgetting
yesterday's tragedy.

Blinded by unreliable sources,
never questioning the credibility.
Screaming at the top of our lungs:
"We care about what's going on."
We don't even care about ourselves.

Fast-food, fast cars, drugs that kill us
faster as chemicals change the color
of our water. On the edge of extinction—
All we care about is our phones
and Wi-Fi connections.

The world will work itself out,
until it crosses over to our own backyard.
Suddenly, everyone has a degree
in political science, spewing hate,
widespread terror and intolerance.

The media pushes it down our throats,
then gives a us a beacon of hope.
Everything will be OKAY.
It wasn't yesterday or the day before,
We don't even know what we're fighting for.

Why should we?
We don't have a clue.
Issues only spark our interest
until the next pop star
does something offensive.

We have ADD and a selective memory,
Peace doesn't sell, sex does,
We have a voice for a split second,
We use it to talk about nothing,
and nowhere is where we're going.

The First Day I Met My Love

The lump in my throat. Can't count how any times I asked for directions. Parking my car in a seedy part of town, sweat on the back of my neck, walking up the steps to her apartment door. Never meeting in person before, only exchanging words through a dating website, not much to go on other than what we both looked like. We had been talking a couple of months, awaiting the encounter.

To say she stole my heart at a first glance would not be true. Average looking, standing at 5'2", but friendly enough with a great smile and body language lighting up the room. I was a mess. Sweating, and unable to control the social anxiety that had crippled me for years. She asked why I was shaking. I made up something about my sugar dropping. We sat, made chit-chat.

Watched a movie, some chick-flick with Ben Affleck. Wasn't my cup of tea, but she was very sweet and seemed comfortable. It became apparent very quickly that I was more scared of her than she was of me. Leaving her place that night, not knowing where it would go, but with the feeling if anything I had made a friend. Though opposites, we attracted, and I gained the best friend I had ever known.

A Life with Regret

We forget the sins we've
committed, memory dormant
though unforgiving,
never speaking of them,
hoping to be washed clean.

The recurring nightmares,
can't imagine the ones
she woke to. Who hit who first—
inconsequential. The night
forever stains my subconscious.

Broken nose, concussed,
charges never filed.
I wish I had done time,
deserving nothing less,
losing myself in the madness.

I'll never be clean again.

My Utopia

Alignment.
The touch, only slightly
perceptible. The rose,
wilting, knows
nothing of its own mortality.

The man,
altering his conscious
frame of mind, breathes heavily.
In
and
out.
Knowing nothing
of his own morality.

Once ignorant,
the man now sees things filtered,
proceeding with vigilance.
He opens his eyes
and his mind.

Cause and Effect

To right? Flight? Vandalize?
Cause or consequence,
whatever chosen, repercussion.
Choosing a positive kills something
negative that could have happened.

Fueling and motivating,
through my spite, I write. Or I fight.
Scars remain from injuries sustained,
Post-Concussion Syndrome,
blackened eyes and broken hand.

Choosing paths of glory or of wrath,
One action destroys the possibility
of another from being, do nothing
and wait for the coming—
I have waited too long.

It could be a definitive decision,
making the difference in a war
that could have been prevented,
Just a choice, nothing more, nothing less.
Wish upon a star or leave it to your god.

Indigo

Indigo.
Dressed from head
to toe, painted blue,
a cartoon; a parody
of what I was.

The song, woeful
and familiar, plays
on repeat in my head,
a constant reminder:
I'm not anywhere yet.

I'll get there eventually,
Maybe I won't leave
the house, sleep for days,
take my pills, drift away.
Comatose.

Blind Rage
(Inspired by the comic book character Daredevil.)

Held captive by darkness,
the TV, flashing nonsense
at high volumes, digital
hi-fi surround sound—
distortion.

Intense white-noise assists
in making out the shadows,
focus is sharp, clear.
Concentration and training keeps
me in peak physical condition.

Man without fear.

Bloody from last night's war,
sight a distraction I can't afford,
I'd give anything to see the sky one
last time. Pink and orange sunrises,
sunsets offset by bluish-purple.

The Devil, resting on his throne,
eyelids closing—no time for sleep.
Nodding off, I hear their screams
in perfect unison. A heartbeat
echoing in rhythm.

The Great Debate

Open your heart—
No consideration, I'm looking
down. You, up. The things
we cannot change, arguing
our irrelevant point
of views. The attack.

Quoting books not fully
understood—words have worth.
Speaking with conviction,
not listening for the nuances
in each other's voice.
Hurt.

Distractions making
scathing noises, desperately
trying to communicate
by seeing who can speak
the loudest,
Who carries the biggest stick.

The Legacy

The renaissance man;
not a poet, a voice.
Nothing to get off his chest,
legacy sound in the question
he poses to ask.

The poet,
melancholy in his rhetorical attribution,
writes timeless and immortal
words, legacy unnoticed,
death.

The artist,
a peddler and a pauper,
creative entrepreneur,
ahead of his time,
a failed concept.

Into the Void

The young insomniac
dreams his life away,
Subsisting on condiments,
suppressing memories
of the past.

Fighting to stay awake,
he challenges his illusions,
Vigilantly searching for answers
to the questions
he's afraid to ask.

Elusive is the voice
he is denied. Reason.
Eyes straining,
pulled back into the void.

Wake up.

Capitol Street

Capitol Street,
I am the king, owning the city
for what it's worth,
Two blocks down.

Change of scenery,
dive bars to pretentious art fags,
cultured, knowing nothing
of my world.

Ostentatious, percolating their lattes,
herbal teas, formal degrees.
I too went to school,
educated by unforgiving streets.

Where is the acceptance?
Ostracized, I carry on,
archangels lifting me,
flying me to where I need to go:

Eden.

The Pupil and The Teacher

Words, combated in silence.
Vision slurred, the intensity.
With patience of a stone,
eyes demanding the utmost accord.

The pupil and his teacher acting
in perfect unison. The greatest
sense of perception,
comprehension.

I looked into the old man's gaze.
It was a privilege. Looking back,
he never asked me to be anything.
Man with no boundaries.

Duality

Psychosis,
playing the victim,
No more in control of your
addictions than the duality
of your actions,
Spiraling down, damning
everyone that cares.

The paradigm shifts:
the false sense of entitlement,
the temper.
You've cheated death
so many times,
your violent crimes were met
with a slap on the wrist.

I believe you would have killed me;
psychologically raping me,
I've forgiven you, only to watch
you destroy your life and the lives
of everyone who cares for you simultaneously.
Goodbye old friend.
Goodbye.

Coward with a Golden Heart

I can't bring myself to turn on the news,
A recluse, removing myself
from the world revolving
around me. Too much animosity,
erupting on all sides of my aura.

The obsession, the oppression,
empathy makes my head bleed.
Cursed to feel the pain
from my friends
and from people I've never met.

I want to make a difference,
to reach people, to move them.
My art is all I have to give.
No more relevant than a flaccid
old man, lonely and nostalgic.

Watching my delusions dissipate
before my eyes, I thought I could
save the world. I can't save myself.
Afraid to leave the house,
coward with a golden heart.

The Future is History

The sun burned out, fading desolate rock. Titanium ships equipped with artillery and rationed supplies, soaring the cosmos, leaving our home behind. The new world, much like the old-altering climates and diplomatic governments, elected officials and technologies allowing us to cultivate. For hundreds of years, we raised our children, building cities rich with art and Utopian laws. Our armies defending us from alien invasions. The new law allowed certain freedoms, regulations put in place to ensure the well-being of the tribe. Curfews and conservative views, religions based off of primitive folklore, prisons built for those who didn't comply.

Over time, radicals and freethinkers threatening to destroy the way of the land were hunted, incarcerated, and ultimately exiled. The rebels gathered in huts, seventy miles from Shangri-La. A truce made, they would survive in the wastelands, eating only what they could kill. They sniffed out the lowest life-forms on the planet, clavicles showing from malnourishment, laying waste in the harsh desert-like environment.

The attacks began on the fourth hour of the second moon, terrorists hitting hard, a military barrage. Civilization crumbled while those in power planned their retreat. On the ninth hour, titanium ships equipped with artillery and rationed supplies, soared the cosmos, leaving their home behind.

The Shadow

Exit the garden,
cast into the storm,
Wretched trees,
apathy.

Goaded into the pit,
shadowed by the son,
Morning eclipsed
by the divide.

Nonconformity deceives
the tribe. Angel radiating
brilliant white light.
Tragedy.

I no longer am defined
by the shadow. My guise,
perceived by mortal eyes
and bona fide lies, is free.

The Hero

The classroom?
The hall?
I was young, my memory is shot.
It was at school where I saw
a train wreck. Flying teeth,
ongoing cheers from insensitive peers,
The blood enough to drown in three
times over. Puddle under the boy's head so deep,

A crime scene.

St. Albans West Virginia
before we were "Meth Town USA,"
before the mines were closing,
Before kids texted or before PC.
Two kids got into a fight, nothing to see—
I couldn't turn away. Kids took bets
on the winner like a dog at the races,
I'd be lying if I said I didn't partake.

Everyone instigates.

The bigger one, after breaking the smaller
one's nose, wrestled him to the ground,
landing multiple head-butts.
The crowd roared, salivating,
watching him continue to pulverize
the already-weakened skull.
A sudden sense of urgency
pulsated through my body,
Surrounded by unintelligible classmates.

What could I do?

I always told myself, if the situation presented
itself, I could be a hero, push people
out of the way of moving vehicles.
Conflicted.
Mercifully, two teachers pulled the brute

31

off the kid on the floor,
eyes rolling into his head.
An ambulance on its way.
If I had it to do it over,

Would I have been the hero?

I try not to lose any sleep over it,
A typical fight, no one died,
The kid on top got expelled,
The one on the bottom
did homeschool.

I think about that day,
teachers flipping the boy over,
keeping him from drowning in his own blood.
The chants in the hall, stains on the wall.
A typical fight,
Like so many after
and so many before.

Act of Human Kindness

Hey man, need a hand?
Looks like you've got
a lot on your plate. I can't relate,
but I've had my share of rainy days.

Hey ma'am, need a ride?
Going down that road anyways,
It's getting late, two miles isn't out
of the way, no need to offer me pay.

The reimbursement, the expressions,
the emotions, the satisfaction.
It wasn't until what I'm doing for you
was done for me that I understood
the magnitude.

Not about religion or self-indulgence.
Not a hero by definition,
just trying to make a difference.

A dent, to scratch the surface,
won't be let down by the look in
their eyes, an indescribable thing
to witness—
the act of human kindness.
The most fulfilling thing you can
do is not bother with subtle nuances.
It is its own reward.